CREATURE CRAFTS

PETS

Annalees Lim

WAYLAND

CONTENTS

Welcome to the wonderful world of
pets!

Do you have a pet? Or is there perhaps a pet that you would really like to own? This book not only shows you how to make your very own crafty pets, it also tells you lots of fun facts about them along the way!

Follow the easy step by step instructions to start creating your own pet collection. When you have finished making an animal, you can also think about how it is kept and looked after.

A lot of the projects use paint and PVA glue. Always cover surfaces with a piece of plastic or layers of old newspaper. Whenever you can, leave the project to dry before moving on to the next step. This avoids things getting stuck to each other or paint smudging.

So, do you have your craft tools at the ready? Then get set to make your crafty creatures and discover what makes each of them so special!

You can even follow QR codes to watch videos of how some of the crafts are made!

HAMSTER IN A WHEEL

You will need:
Empty cheese box
White A5 paper
Orange and brown crayons
Wooden tooth pick
Glue stick
Scissors
Paper fastener
Grey felt tipped pen
White A4 card
Red paper
Googly eyes
Black marker pen

Hamsters usually sleep in the day and play at night. But this hamster will be ready to spin in its wheel all day long!

1

Colour the A5 sheet of white paper in a layer of orange crayon. Then cover that layer completely with brown crayon.

2

Scratch off some of the brown crayon using the wooden tooth pick. Make the scratches look like fur.

3

Use a black marker pen to draw a hamster shape, making sure your include small ears and legs. Cut out your hamster. Stick on the googly eyes with a glue stick.

4

Cut out a circle of red paper that is bigger than the cheese box. Stick the circle to the middle of the white A4 card. Cut out a red paper triangle to form the base of the wheel.

5

Use the grey felt tipped pen to draw spokes onto the wheel. Fix it to the middle of the red circle with the paper fastener. Glue the hamster to the wheel.

HAMSTER FACT
Did you know that hamsters can use pouches in their cheeks to store food?

POM-POM CHINCHILLA

You will need:
Grey wool
A4 card
Compass
Pencil
Scissors
Ruler
Dark and light grey felt
Fabric glue
Googly eyes

Chinchillas live high up in the mountains. They have very soft, thick fur. Make your craft chinchilla just as fluffy by using soft wool.

1

Fold the A4 card in half. Draw a 5cm-wide circle, then a 15cm-wide circle around it. Cut around the edge of the large circle to make 2 card circles. Fold the circles in half and cut the inside circle out of each of them.

2

Make a paper bobbin out of scrap card. Wrap some grey wool around it, making sure it does not get bigger than the holes in the circles.

3

Place one circle on top of the other and start wrapping the wool around them. Make sure there are no gaps in the wool and that you wind 3 layers in total.

4

Carefully slide the scissors between the card circles and cut the wool around the edge. Wind a length of wool between both circles, pull it tight and tie a knot. Remove the card.

5

Cut out ears, a nose, front and back paws, and a tail from the felt. Stick them to the pom-pom with the fabric glue. Glue on the googly eyes.

CHINCHILLA FACT
A chinchilla's teeth never stop growing! They need to gnaw on wood to keep their teeth short.

POSH POODLE

You will need:
- A4 card
- Black marker pen
- Cotton wool balls
- Paint
- Pot of water
- Fabric glue
- Glitter glue
- Plastic bowl
- Paintbrush
- Scissors

Poodles are not just pretty to look at. They are one of the most intelligent dog breeds, too. Make your very own smart poodle to impress your friends!

1

Mix equal amounts of the paint and water in a bowl.

2

Soak 8 cotton wool balls in the paint mixture. Take them out and leave them to dry.

3

Use the black marker pen to draw the shape of a poodle on the A4 card. Draw the face, two legs and the tail, leaving space for the body and head.

4

Stick the cotton wool balls onto the card using the fabric glue. They will form the ears, body, tail-end and cuffs. You can make some smaller balls by cutting them up.

5

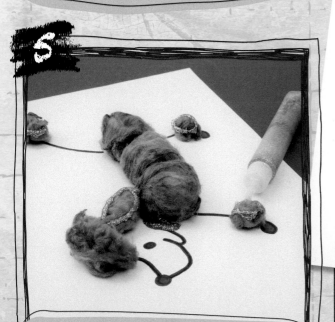

Decorate your poodle with glitter glue. Don't forget to add a collar, too.

POODLE FACT
Ancient Greeks used to keep pet poodles thousands of years ago!

GOOGLY-EYED GOLDFISH

You will need:
Transparent plastic tub
3 x small balloons
Orange tissue paper
Googly eyes
Modelling clay
Green tissue paper
Small stones
PVA glue, glue stick
Bowl of water
Paintbrush
Toothpicks
Scissors
Ruler

Goldfish are happiest when they are in a group. Make these goldfish to go in your tank so that they can keep each other company.

1

Mix equal amounts of water and PVA glue in a bowl. Blow up 3 balloons so they are no bigger than 7 cm long.

2

Tear the orange tissue paper into small strips and dip each one into the PVA–water mix. Stick them on the balloons until you have 3 layers of tissue paper. Leave to dry in a warm place.

3

When the tissue paper has dried, pop the balloons inside. Add some more tissue paper to each balloon to make fins and tails. Stick a pair of googly eyes to each fish.

4

Cut wavy shapes out of the green paper. Stick them around the inside of the plastic tub using a glue stick.

GOLDFISH FACT

Goldfish have great memories. This means it's possible to train a goldfish to do little tricks!

5

Press 3 chunks of modelling clay onto the bottom of the tub. Pierce the goldfish with toothpicks and stand them up in the modelling clay. Add small stones to the tub.

Watch this video of how to make your goldfish!

BUBBLE WRAP LIZARD

You will need:
Bubble wrap
Glass paints
Scissors
A4 sheet of paper
Pencil
Paintbrush
Thick, coloured card
Glue stick

A lizard's skin is not slimy, as you might think. It's very dry, and it is often bright and colourful. Use your favourite colours to decorate your lizard's skin.

1 Using a pencil, draw a lizard shape onto the paper to make a template. Cut it out with scissors.

2 Paint a pattern onto the bubble wrap using lots of different colours of glass paint. Leave to dry completely before moving on to the next step.

Stick the template to the bubble wrap and carefully cut around the lizard shape.

Cut a lizard shape that is a bit bigger than your template out of the thick, coloured card.

Stick the bubble wrap lizard onto the coloured card using a glue stick.

LIZARD FACT
If lizards lose their tail when they are being hunted, they can grow a new one!

FLUFFY BUNNY

Rabbits are born with their eyes closed and without fur. This fluffy bunny has its eyes wide open, lots of fur and is only slightly smaller than a real-life bunny!

1

Fold one of the white dusters in half. Fold the left edge towards the middle.

2

Fold the right edge over to the left side of the duster.

3

Roll the ends of the folded duster towards each other. Tightly wrap a length of white string around it and secure with a strong knot. This will form your bunny's body.

4

Tie off two corners of the other duster, using white string. These will form your bunny's ears. Roll the rest of the duster together in a tight ball. Tie the ears together using ribbon.

5

Use fabric glue to stick your bunny's head to its body. Stick the pom-pom on to form the tail. Glue on the googly eyes and a nose cut out of pink felt.

BUNNY FACT
Rabbits can jump higher and further than a lot of humans can!

Watch this video of how to make your bunny!

15

BEADY SNAKE

Some snakes can grow up to 9 metres long! You can make your snake as long as you like. Be sure to choose colourful fabric, too.

You will need:
30cm x 6cm fabric
Lots of small beads (no wider than 2cm)
Fabric glue
Embroidery thread
Red felt
Scissors
2 x small black beads
Measuring tape

1

Make a tube from the fabric and stick in place with the fabric glue. Also glue one end closed and leave to dry completely before moving on to the next step.

2

Put a few beads inside the fabric tube and tie a length of thread around the tube to hold them in place.

3

Repeat this for the rest of the tube until you have 3cm of fabric left. Trim the end of the tube.

4

Wrap scrap fabric around a bead to form your snake's head. Tie the fabric together using embroidery thread. Glue the head to the body of your snake.

5

Cut out a tongue from the red felt and stick it to the head, using the fabric glue. Stick the black beads onto the side of the head to form your snake's eyes.

SNAKE FACT

Did you know that snakes can't chew? This means that they have to swallow their food whole!

FEATHERY BUDGIE

Budgies have about 2,000–3,000 feathers! You can use just a handful to make your own colourful pet bird.

1

Cut and bend each of the pipe cleaners to form a leg and claws. Stick them into the bottom of the polystyrene egg, so that it stands up.

2

Paint the egg in a layer of blue paint and leave it to dry.

3

Glue feathers to each side of the egg to make wings.

4

Cut out two yellow triangles, one slightly bigger than the other. Fold each triangle in half and then stick them onto the egg to form the beak.

5

Glue some googly eyes above your budgie's beak.

BUDGIE FACT
Did you know that budgies can learn how to say words and phrases?

PLAYFUL KITTEN

Kittens learn how to hunt by playing with their brothers and sisters. You can make your very own kitten that plays with a ball of wool!

1

Cut an 'H' shape out of orange foam. Make sure that the outline of the 'H' is 7cm wide and 15cm tall.

2

Cut out a 20cm x 7cm rectangle of orange foam for the body. Cut out a wavy shape that is 10cm tall to form the tail.

3

Shape the rectangle to form a tube and staple it together. Staple the 'H' shape to the tube and staple the tail to the bottom of the 'H'.

4

Bend the 4 lengths of the 'H' around the tube and staple them in place. Round off the ends of the lengths with scissors.

5

Make your kitten's face from foam and stick it together using PVA glue. Glue the face to the top of the tube. You can also stick pink pads of foam to its paws. Place a ball of wool between its paws.

CAT FACT
Did you know that cats sleep a lot more than we do? They nap for about 18 hours a day!

PUG POTS

You will need:
3 x toilet roll tubes
20cm x 10cm thick, coloured card
Brown, cream, and white paper
Glue stick
Scissors
Black felt tipped pen

In ancient China, pugs used to sit on the laps of emperors. You can make pug pots to sit on your desk and hold your pens!

1

Cut 2 toilet rolls so that they are different heights - one should be a bit shorter than the other.

2

Cover both cut rolls in cream paper. Cover the full-length roll in brown paper.

3

Make lots of small cuts into one end of each tube. Splay the ends out and stick the tubes onto the coloured card.

4

Cut out two cream 'U' shapes and one brown 'U' shape. Cut out 4 small, cream-coloured paws and 2 brown ones. Stick the shapes and paws to a pot of the same colour.

5

Make a pug face for each of your pots by cutting out shapes from the coloured paper. Use your felt tipped pen to add details. Stick each face onto a pot of the same colour.

PUG FACT
Pugs have short noses. This means that they catch colds very easily.

GLOSSARY

bobbin   an object that has thread or wool wound around it

emperor   a man who rules over a group of countries

intelligent   when a human or an animal is able to understand and learn things very well

template   a shape that is used as a guide to cut out something

INDEX

First published in 2015 by Wayland

Copyright © Wayland 2015

Wayland
338 Euston Road
London NW1 3BH

Wayland Australia
Level 17/207 Kent Street
Sydney NSW 2000

Wayland, part of Hachette Children's Group and published
by Hodder and Stoughton Limited
www.hachette.co.uk

Series editor: Julia Adams
Craft photography: Simon Pask, N1 Studios
Additional images: Shutterstock

Dewey classification: 745.5-dc23
ISBN: 9780750284462
ebook ISBN: 9780750293785

Printed in China

The QR codes included in this book were valid at the time of
going to press. However, because of the nature of the Inter-
net, it is possible that addresses may have changed, or sites
may have changed or closed down, since publication.

Get your paws on all the books in the Creature Crafts series!

978 0 7502 8448 6

978 0 7502 8447 9

978 0 7502 95543 7

978 0 7502 8446 2

978 0 7502 8449 3

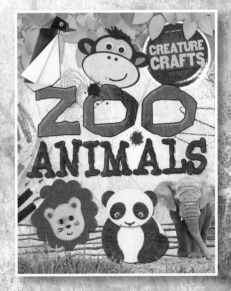

978 0 7502 9544 4